CITIES *of* FLESH

and

THE DEAD

Cover art: "Sanctuary" by Peter Goodwin

Book design by Joel A. Bass

ISBN: 978-1-932-41826-2

Elixir Press
PO Box 27029
Denver, Colorado 80227

www.ElixirPress.com

Elixir Press is a nonprofit literary organization.

CITIES *of* FLESH *and* THE DEAD

POEMS

Diann Blakely

ELIXIR PRESS

to my friends,
here, and still here

Grateful acknowledgment is made to the publications in which these poems originally appeared, sometimes in earlier versions and/or with different titles:

American Literary Review ("Christmas: Ext., Wide-Angle," "Antonioni's *Blow-Up*" from *Home Movies*), **Antioch Review** ("Bad Blood," also in **Pushcart Prize Anthology XX**; "Before the Flood: A Solo from New Orleans," "The Triumph of Style"), **BOMB** ("On the Border"), **Chelsea** ("'Installation,' Warhol Museum" from *Home Movies*), **Colorado Review** (*Blood Oranges*), **Crab Orchard Review** (*The Last Violet*), **Denver Quarterly** ("Half-Day Bus Tour, 2004," "Steward of the Signet Society, 1985" from *Home Thoughts from Abroad*), **Green Mountains Review** ("'A Fool in Love,' 1960," "On Tour with the Stones, 1966," "Nutbush and Ripley" from *Sonnets for Tina: A Call and Response*), **Image** ("The Pink Palace" from *Home Movies*), **The Journal** ("Music City Duet"), **Nebraska Review** (*Manhattan Love Stories: From the Millennium*), **New England Review** ("Memphis Blues"), **Parnassus** ("Objects of Desire"), *Crossroads: Newsletter of the Poetry Society of America* ("Afterwords"), **Prairie Schooner** ("Reunions: Kensington, 2004," "Announcements: Jackson Boulevard 1967 and 1980" from **Home Thoughts from Abroad**), **Puerto del Sol** ("Tina in her Garden: Los Angeles," "At the Tuckers: Ripley, Tennessee," "Duet at the Girls' School" from *Sonnets for Tina: A Call and Response*), **Triquarterly** ("St. Louis, 1958," "Gimme Shelter, 1970," "Re-Watching *Tommy*" from *Sonnets for Tina: A Call and Response*), **Vanderbilt Review** ("Antidepressive"), **Yale Review** ("Matinées"), **Witness** (*Church of Jesus with Signs Following*)

The author wishes to thank, in addition to the dedicatees in these pages, Molly Bendall, Anne Doolittle, Ben Downing, Anne Reeves, Margaret Renkl, David St. John, Bruce Smith, and Bill Wadsworth, for critical, and often crucial, encouragement and support.

Very special appreciation to Tree Swenson and the Academy of American Poets and to Baron Wormser and the Poetry Society of America. And, also, to Dana Curtis and Sarah Kennedy.

While the places in this book are real, some of the characters and scenes within their borders should be understood as fictions.

Introduction

A new collection by Diann Blakely always promises entrance to a tragic, beautiful world. Combining controlled prosody and extravagant aesthetic, Blakely makes sonnets, dramatic monologues, and lyrics that, in rough iambic pentameter lines, render the gritty details of Southern girlhood. These particulars, tempered by sensitivity to emotional and linguistic nuance and harnessed by form, have always been features of her work, and *Cities of Flesh and the Dead* pushes the lyric first-person narrative at which Blakely has always excelled to include historical personae and interlinked sequences. Attentive, careful, and self-reflexive, these poems create a palimpsest of the contemporary South, where the present is always complicated by the haunting voices of the past.

The movies and TV figure in several of the poems, beginning with the first poem, "Bad Blood," in which *Psycho* becomes the touchstone for viewers. Anthony Perkins is "the actor [who] embodie[s] our worst fears" and Hollywood is the scene of collective American desire to be saved from aging and death. Ireland, which figures largely in the imaginations of many Americans, is both an ideal tourist destination and a source of frightening political tension. Visiting Northern Ireland and driving into the Republic, the narrator in "'Whatever You Say, Say Nothing,'" is confronted by the signs of bloodshed and feels "Glad though half-ashamed of the minor surge of fear / That disperses my travellers' fog." Those mixed emotions resolve into the elegiac mode of "'The Last Violet,'" a sequence written in the voice of Mary Jane Kelly, the Irish woman who was the last known victim of Jack the Ripper. In "Objects of Desire," an unrelenting longing to be lovingly looked at, like "Vivien/Blanche" in *A Streetcar Named Desire*, collides with the frustration and pain such craving breeds; the narrator remembers her mother curling her hair to make her *"pretty / As a princess"* while burning her ears.

Popular media and popular legend bleed into personal and family history in the course of this book. The sonnet sequence "Manhattan Love Stories: From the Millenium," written in memory of Lynda Hull, traces the friendship between the poets through remembered song lyrics, poems, visual art, and tattoos. The series, dedicated to her "sweet gone friend," traces the sadness that pervades the entire book. To remember the late twentieth century in America is also to recall "siren screams," "Abortion, cancer, AIDS, divorce," tranquilizers, and the disappearance of a student who found "swastikas drawn on her locker." She dismisses her own younger self as "Laughable / At best," full of "small suburban fears and shames." But she also recognizes with a terrifying clarity that childhood, with its inevitable misery, is less funny when seen in terms of its propulsion of us all into "messy" adulthood, where we all engage in constructing "our fumbled histories."

History is, indeed, plural in *Cities of Flesh and the Dead*. Memories of her mother screaming, "'I hate babies—they mess up your nice things,'" intersect with memories of a husband "trampling down the Yorkshire dales" without her; dates appear out of chronological order, while the suicide of Sylvia Plath and the marriage of "Tom and Viv" bump up against each other in the narrator's imagination. This "childless daughter" leaves her mother in a hotel room and ends up in St. Paul's, by happenstance standing with a group of German tourists, and in the cacophony of languages, asks for "blessing in [her] mother tongue."

But any blessing is transient in Blakely's world. Aware of the instability of our personal narratives and impatient with self-aggrandizement—"Aren't you bored / With those family scenes, replayed so many times? / And 'Dantescan' and 'surviving'—can't you find words / / Less grandiose?"—she also knows that the self is made up of such gestures. "You know about the singer's husband," the narrator of "Home Movies" states, "dead now for years, / / Another suicide, MTV still haunted / By his ashen junkie's face, by barbed-wire guitar licks / And shots of his little girl, who dances frenzied / / On legs as plump as yours were kicking in red socks." The two images are inextricably entwined in the complicated making of a self, along with movie images, photos of Jackie Onassis and Marilyn Monroe, and stories about Anne Sexton. A seashell, itself not a simple thing but a commodity, a "souvenir," becomes the sign of this pastiche-self; she holds it to her ear, and "the roar slips / Those fragile borders . . . / which pulse like the world" ("Home Movies").

A slipping of borders may best characterize the troubling and beautiful poems of this book. Nowhere—neither in her native South with the hypocrisy and weirdness of its expressions of Christian faith nor in other cities where danger and dislocation always threaten—does the speaker feel at home. Chicago is unexpectedly warm in "mid-February," and the narrator's "drawled requests" mark her as an outsider among the Midwestern natives. The city in "Solo, New Orleans" is a shock, and she arrives "not expecting haze / Heat already swathing the smelly narrow streets." In "Memphis Blues," the narrator is as out of place, "even more alien," in her own Tennessee as the other tourists, and the persistent problem of racial violence adds to her sense of displacement. And yet, the shared culture of music, art, books, and movies ties her to other women, to other Americans, and to the larger world: "God," this poet asks, "what forms can / Love take except the smudged, the failed, the human?"

Sarah Kennedy

Table of Contents

I

Exiles and Returns

Voi ch'entrate, and your life is in your hands.
Robert Lowell

BAD BLOOD

A woman stares, wild-eyed from the terror known only when death,
      That black-winged angel,
Appears without warning, without any time for prayers, rescue,
      Or bargains; appears
As a sinking car, as a plane arrowing a thousand feet
      Per second; appears
As a murderer's knife, unsheathed and glittering. Her wet blond hair,

Grayish in the black-and-white film, drips at the sides of her face
      And emphasizes
Those eyes, that darkly lipsticked mouth shaped in a scream's darker *o*.
      Blood spatters the tile
Then the cracked drain, its perforations flooding with stained water.
      Flashbacks to *Psycho*:
What middle-ager doesn't succumb, at least in motel showers,

Recalling these shots, or Bates straitjacketed while a fly roams
      His twitching fingers?
A man too gentle to hurt a fly, the voice-over repeats.
      With brute surrender,
The actor embodied our worst fears: like dying in the bath—
      Or flames, or black winds—
Trusting water like a lover to soothe, to cleanse off the grit

And smudge of ill-spent pasts, to give us a new starts. No new start
      For a man offered
Only crazed killer roles in his short life, who quoted a film
      In his dying days.
An easier story: everyone knew Germans were the bad guys,
      That Ingrid Bergman's
Suffering was noble, though her career was nearly sunk by—

Living in sin? out-of-wedlock kids? One era's moral rage
      Turns ash as quickly
As the next shapes its fears. *Keep me safe, keep me safe*—we repeat
      Craven litanies now,
In time of plagues, want to feel singled out and cherished by God,

Who'll surely spare us,
Our friends, our families. Almost sensual, these open-mouthed pleas

For blessing, as when we let water sluice its warm passage down
        Our flesh at the end
Of a day that's pummeled us into exhaustion and blankness,
        When we drop our hands
To unbutton a shirt, pull on the harsh teeth of a zipper,
        Look in someone's eyes
And pray *love me, treasure my body, don't ever let me die.*

FAMILY BATTLES

1. Christmas 1964

My uncle stares at the TV throughout
Our midday feast, erupts with "Fucking Krauts"
Three times, which I'll repeat on the way home
And be spanked, my Barbie taken from me.
We didn't often see my father's family;
This sad-faced man, introduced as Eddie,
Spent most months at a VA hospital
Thorazined and crying in the chapel
For his buddies, two decades after the invasion
At Ste Mère Église. There seasickness and waves
Wobbled the Allies' legs as bullets kissed
The sand, as mortars spewed from bunkers hidden
Beneath dunes. Eight men from his platoon survived.
Eddie winks at me and twirls the carving knife.

2. *Sanctuary/Requiem for a Nun*

"St. Mary Magdalene," the rector jokes
As I, dragged to this confirmation class
At dawn, stare dozily through frost-etched windows,
"Is often the girls' favorite . . ." A few blush
At his strange opener; and then I'm passed,
From knees beneath the table, a book one kid
Has filched from home: vein-tangled, sweaty breasts—
Their black bra too—adorn the jacket spread
For Faulkner's tale of Temple Drake. A belle
Turned whore, she's transformed by loss and contrition
When her child dies.". . . Because hairdressers call
On Mary as"—his chilblained right hand stretched
Toward my bent shag—"their patron slut . . . er, saint."
Free me, O Lord, to burn, or freeze, and pay.

3. Sewanee: 25th College Reunion, 2004

The cornerstone, now thickly choked with weeds
And fallen leaves, is easy to miss—
I scout the path with my flashlight, alert
For snakes. The chapel's bells strike ten; their tower,
Like the black gowns we wore flapping to class,
Pay homage to Oxbridge, which gathered funds
To rebuild a college burned by Union troops:
Those mills belching smoke in Yorkshire landscapes
Would have starved without cheap Dixie cotton.
An antique chest, earrings, some hand-cut glass—
Freed by remains of a maternal dower,
I joined the few girls allowed here, too smart
Not to learn to surrender when amiss
In history class, where home wars rarely bleed.

"WHATEVER YOU SAY, SAY NOTHING"

No lark, no making light of bombs and kneecappings,
This detour through Derry: according to the map,
A2's the shortest route to the Sligo cottage
Where we've reserved a room. How peaceful it appears
In the glossy brochure's shots: windows wreathed with roses,
And a bay view. Tired, we've just toured Inoshowen,

That rock-strewn jut into the Atlantic; no buffer
Between us and the Pole but ocean, we stood in gorse,
The wind stinging my skin, and turned *south* to view Ulster,
An idea so odd you dropped my hand and gouged
Two shapes in sand to explain it. With little coaxing,
I take the wheel, try to adjust the driver's seat,

Glad though half-ashamed of the minor surge of fear
That disperses my travellers' fog. Too much Guinness,
Salt gales and wave-riven shorelines. Our fight last night.
The border crossing's easy, almost a disappointment,
And the city could be any industrial one back home,
Except for its burned-out, windowless rowhouses,

Their bullet-pocked stone walls. Then, on a street whose yards
Are edged with flowers, like our own, soldiers appear:
Cradling rifles, they march in step then pirouette;
Their helmeted, shadowy eyes check left, check right,
What might come at their backs. A routine patrol,
You say, but knock my hand away from the lighter:

Could a lit cigarette look like a threat? The Foyle
Comes into view, and still I put off smoking; the thrill
Of our small dare has dulled, and I'm eager to leave.
Should we have proof, you ask, pointing to roadblocks
Then the backseat, where our loaded camera sits.
The shutter's scarcely closed when guards step from a booth,

Its bulletproof glass sides festooned with razor wire;
People like us just make things worse—I blush, knowing
The soldier right—and he should confiscate our camera,
Arrest the driver. "You must see our side, sir," he says,
Consonants barbed. "We're under terrorist attack here."
You try to shake his hand. He'll let me go this time,

Waving us toward the Republic; "Donegal-Sligo-Leitrim—
The Friendly Counties" have put up a sign as welcome.
Their hills, mist-softened mounds of postcard-green, rise
To meet us as Derry's smokestacks become tall smudges
In my rear mirror and radio towers grow distant,
Spikes looped together with wire, dividing the sky.

THE LAST VIOLET

Mary Jane Kelly, 1863-1888

1.

Limerick, sir? *Sweet flows the River Shannon,*
Or don't you know that song? I spent girlhood
In neighborhoods more posh than Whitechapel,
Its butcherhouses' stink and rummies slumped
By Maiden Lane, where some woo rougher trade
Then shrink beneath a sweaty fist in rooms
Like this: *o murder's* heard here late at night
Almost as often as St. Mary's bells,
The same cry heard when Jack still wore nappies.
'Tis a comedown for me, raised to paint china,
Embroider silk and linen, taught to sing—
Only a Violet's my favorite—
By mam before she and the last babe died.
My first stop here in London was the same
As all good Irish girls', some glad to scrub
A convent's floors for porridge and a cot,
But who'd call these fair wages? Even here—
Ma maisonette—I keep a lady's ways:
This basin, my bottle of French perfume
And that small one of brandy—there, a nip
Will take the chill November from your bones.
Thieves stole my oil-lamp and the wee portrait
By Walter Sickert, no less, when I took ill
With quinsy, fevered in that infirmary bed.
Now I sleep days after twisting the sheets
With proper husbands in derbies like yours—
Lord's name, are you really a bachelor?—
Who go home late to their wives, long asleep,
Milk-faced and tight-kneed, dreaming of the Queen.

2.

That courtship teaches whoring's mortal shame
But true: young girls trade kisses for bouquets,
Let sweaty hands roam their breasts in return
For tuppence frills and bows. *Only a violet . . .*
I'd fancied marriage more romantic than
A ring and overnight at Cardiff, Davies'
Sod-drunk sleeps soon as he got the mine's pay
And fun from me. E'er dirty, he'd roll off
To snore, and, turning up the lamp, I'd check
For smudges—you, like true gents, look to know
That soap and water won't melt bones. Davies
Died in the explosion that also killed
The dads, who'd dragged us all cross-channel when
Sacked from the Limerick bank: barely nineteen
I was, and left to scrimp for London fare;
Then how I cursed the dads, cursed how he'd drained
My dowry soon as we'd shut poor mam's eyes
With coppers. Roaring he'd be, and gutter-mouthed
At table; my greasy brothers smirked, the lot,
When he'd thunder there was one place besides
The kitchen where a woman was good company.
Only a violet . . . sacking, threats
From the landlord, and sending off Brigid,
Who mam had hired as maid, her cheeks still raw
From Galway winds—she'd blush crimson and drop
Her eyes to the joint when dads was four sheets,
Blush and wait for him to stop laughing at
His own blather and start carving the meat.

3.

The West End house? Two dozen oil lamps dripped
With silk fringe, lovey; bare feet disappeared
Into plush Persian rugs. The men there were
The lot's best, so well-mannered they'd say "sorry"
For coming. You like a good laugh, don't you?
One gent hired me for a full week in Paris,
Six giddy nights with oysters and champagne,
A feather bed. That poor dim James, a fiend
For culture, plucked my elbow in the Louvre—
"Coo now! What you call that?"—and exclaimed loud
By stained church windows, checking his moustache
In Notre Dame's carved font. Its statue of
The Virgin, my name-saint, gave me the shivers;
Though one Sunday when James was still asleep
I skittered in before the eight o'clock
To light a candle for that wee sister
I never held, for mam, even one for
The dads. *Hail Mary, full of grace, blessèd*
Art thou among women and blessèd is . . .
A priest two rows away looked up from prayers
Like I'd raved curses; he startled and made
The cross's sign with his smudged, crookèd fingers
Then backed, black-frocked, through an open door.

4.

"Black Mary," jealous wenches nicknamed me
At the Ten Bells . . . less elegant—or *luxe*—
Than the West End house, but nobody takes
A cut, and I've now regulars who queue
For more than evening pints. *Marie Jeannette,*
I whisper when I miss those nights beside
The Seine; once, the slut most covetous
Heard and began to screech like the banshee—
"Her real name's Mary Jane! 'Black Mary' Jane!"
So loud she screeched, my fellow spilled his ale . . .
Pour us a bit more brandy, there's a love.
I don't deserve "Black Mary," I tell myself
When I look into mirrors, my hair flax-blond
And smile sweet as a girl's, plump as those days
I posed for Walt Sickert; I don't deserve
These filthy walls, no matter what I call them,
Nor deserve waking at dusk to find grey rats
Worrying my naked feet. When in her cups,
My friend Liz brogues away about the kirk
And its free destinations . . "Mary, Marie,
Are you listening to me, lass?" I'll have none
Of a Scot's destinations, I say straight,
But her head bows as she claims the parson
Meant that we're doomed to certain things by God—
"Like our monthlies," she moans. The only time
I'm black-tempered. After, I'm back fluttering
My lashes and silk fan, and with bells on.

5.

A suspect's jailed, but Fleet Street ragmen buzz
Like flies to fresher blood: Queen Vicky's eighth
And chloroformed lie-in a scandal to some:
Is it not women's curse to bring forth babes
In pain? Abortionists sell laudanum,
Which I'd drink every night if my labors
Paid more; now even brandy's seeming dear,
My regulars afraid of Whitechapel,
Afraid old Jack might rip them too! 'Tis kind,
Indeed, for you to walk me from the Bells,
To praise my voice: *Only a violet*
Plucked from my mother's grave—och, the neighbors
Complain at any wee noise, make more fuss
Than alley cats, or that pate-addled drunk
Who's whingeing chorus. . . . The halfpenny candle
Gutters, but lately I've not dared close my eyes
Till the dawn breaks, and still, I suffer dreams—
Your derby might hang there, love, near the bag
And gloves—dreams of that murderous blade yellowed
By candlelight and plunging for my throat,
More like one of Sickert's paintings than real;
And in the worst I bowed to hell's own steel,
Just like back home in Limerick I bowed
To the cross our priest hefted, my head dipped
Ready and willing, belly shrunk from fasts,
Shake-kneed and cunt nun-dry . . . be a good heart
And fetch the quilt. I'd steal peeks at the statue
Of Jesus, the red sword-gash in his side,
Those slender, near-girly legs ankle-crossed
Below blood mingled with pale curls and thorns.

in memoriam Anthony Hecht

MEMPHIS BLUES

On Beale Street at dusk, these dozen tourists' faces—
     New England retirees, say age and accent—
          Are the only white ones except mine, even whiter

Than their crinkled tans; even more alien,
     My nervous quickstep learned during those years
          Up north. The Peabody, rehabbed grande dame

Of Deep South hotels, houses us all, and though
     Two rhapsodize about ceiling-high drapes
          And silk bedspreads, their friend protests her view:

"It looks so dirty," she says, the Mississippi
     Pulsing beyond like a huge brown muscle,
          Like the music here. "Meanest blues in town,"

Proclaims a neon sign next to a pawnshop;
     Panhandlers scatter as police start their sweep,
          Keeping the street safe after decades when

Its song dropped to a whisper—"No Man's Land,"
     Meaning white men. The phrase meant women too,
          Though the young don't believe such warnings, at least

Not my husband's stepsister, who adored blues
     And shocking her family. I want to tell you
          How she met a man here, how they fell in love

And healed to one couple's extent these wounds
     That throb like the ground bass—slurried, whirling,
          Holding riffs the way this river holds silt—

And a voice sliding around a tale of love
     Gone wrong. I want to tell you that times change,
          That they'll be welcomed later at my in-laws',

Her skin white, his black, their kids. . . . But she was shot
    On Beale the month we moved back to Tennessee.
        What friends I left knew of the South came, mostly,

From books and films: *To Kill A Mockingbird,*
    Gone with the Wind. The moonlight-and-magnolias
        Literati, who stayed at the Peabody

In seasons when high cotton waved above
    Black delta soil. "Our country's richest land,
        Also its poorest folks," someone quipped;

And couldn't the region begin its spread on Beale?—
    These fractured sidewalks the tourists now veer from,
        Hungry for ribs, away from Handy's park,

Where the "Memphis Blues" plays each sunset, even
    When the audience is two elderly men
        In ties who pass a quart of malt and tap

Their broganed feet as the sax takes it away,
    Offering us another chance for transport,
        The fallen raptures of this murderous world.

ON THE BORDER

Half-hearted vegetarian, I rinse chicken parts for guests,
        Though I've grown squeamish
Since those childhood summers when I watched Delilah butcher hens,
        Absorbing stories
Of her native bayous, how she was taught to forecast love-woes
        By reading entrails,
To catch a husband by tying wishbones with wire. No wedding

For the Texas teenagers whose tale the radio updates:
        Its Spanish broadcast,
Which I tune into sometimes while cooking, missing whole phrases
        In the gravelly rush
Of fricatives, despite those high school classes decades ago.
        Was he more fluent,
The Brownsville Prep gringo, with his girl, a Chicana believed

Too unassimilated even for teen backtalk and dates?—
        Yet she's testified
To sneaking motel weekends with him, lying to her *madre*,
        Who lighted candles
Each day, if I understand the reporter, thanked the Virgin
        For their new brick house,
So large none shared a bedroom. Maybe, like me, this eldest girl

Was careful, called her boyfriend late at night from a closet's hush,
        The hangers swaying
With jeans and her first communion dress, wrapped and tied in plastic.
        Las degradadas,
They'd called those girls in the mother's home town who let their dresses
        And family names
Be stained with dirt in exchange for kisses. The radio details

How the Texas boy was shot before school in his mom's driveway,
        A garden hose coiled
On the concrete like the snake Delilah, one summer dawn, found
        On the dew-soaked porch,
The same summer I avoided her, stuporous with memories of

17

A tongue's propulsion
As I'd swayed backward in a boy's grasp till my hair almost brushed

My soon dirt-stained jeans. Swayed like *la madre* when the Virgin spoke,
        Ordering death to him
Who'd made her daughter *la degradada*. Blood pooled on concrete,
        Also soaked through sheets
When I spread my legs one night, and Delilah never warned me
        Just how much this hurt
Or just how quickly I'd flee that boy; yet part of me believes

That love exists to cross borders, slip into other bodies
        With the same sweet ease
That we slip into sun-warmed grass or a river's muddy flow.
        Or stretch our hands toward—
The stars? dim candle-flickers? the wet warmth of impatient eyes?—
        And gasp as wire stings
And rips our flesh, wire saying *Do Not Enter*, saying *Go Back.*

II

Blood Oranges

MANHATTAN LOVE STORIES: FROM THE MILLENIUM

1. Queensborough Bridge

Four fuming lanes of cars and taxis snake
Stalled from the intersection to farther
Than I can see; the driver's sweaty neck
Cranes out the side window, Black 47
Blasting immigrant rage from a cassette.
He settles back and shouts details of friends
Left behind in Cork, the tape now Costello;
"This is hell, this is hell," lyrics sweetly crooned,
As though he sang of heaven—"but you'll get used
To it . . . it'll never get better or worse"—
Or of this gridlocked traffic, cops short-fused
And bullhorning about an ambulance:
"Again, again," the siren screams; red lights
Flame the window. I'll never get used to it.

2. Itinerary

What's "mid-life" when every long distance call
And letter seem to shriek sad news or loss—
Abortion, cancer, AIDS, divorce; a car crash
That locks me sobbing in school bathroom stalls
Several times a week, though my colleagues
Grow less patient with each new month of tears;
Another friend's psychosis, one's eyes scarred
Near blindness—and some not even thirty?
Two years ago this spring, before L. bought
That rattletrap she died in, she took to pieces
A new poem I'd crowed about, its subject
A loved city: "Dull, distanced . . . what's the reason
You've left home? Girl, why don't you just say it?—
You're choking there. You need to breathe again."

3. Houston Street Grille

Some gulp a tranquilizer when nervous;
My backpack's crammed with three vintage dresses
Costing more than airfare and my room combined,
Bought wildly on the morning's walk downtown.
At home, I'd sworn that our long-tended flame
Was dying low, another habit, shameful,
If less scorned here than post-lunch cigarettes.
Outside, punk lovers, young as my students
But tattooed, jostle my pack-laden arm
While we hug goodbye, their bare ones adorned
With portraits of Charles Manson and Hitler.
Why do these encounters possess such allure
When short, their farewells always chaste, like this?
He'll marry soon—I'll miss him, more or less.

4. Travel Permission

A day off from my prep school's hard to get—
All girls, taught mostly by females, most smart
Yet raised to be fulfilled with love, with friends,
To scant Milton and history for the heart.
The handbook lists our phone numbers; the girls
May call us anytime. And do. (We worry
When they don't.) A substitute's long-scheduled;
I type instructions for the VCR,
An intro for the Sylvia Plath tape,
Tidy my desk. Hours before the plane takes off
The phone rings, and a mom stutters my name:
Her child's been gone all week, but swastikas
Drawn on her locker were the cause, not flu.
Her best theme, on Anne Frank, misspelled *Dachau*.

5. Lost, with L.

My arms shake off the brief imprint of his
On this long stroll back toward the hotel, my knees
Weakening more from pedestrian fatigue
Than regret or loss. Mid-afternoon passes
And even those silk dresses grow heavy
In sudden rain; and am I seeing things?—
Here street signs' letters squiggle, as if leaking,
And everyone seems shorter, their hair inky . . .
Beneath an awning hung with plump chickens,
I rummage for my map and glasses—Christ!
I've walked two miles in the wrong direction.
First anger, then I have to laugh, and then—
I know this place somehow—from another life?
From your Chinatown poems, my sweet gone friend.

6. Woman #5, #18, and #21

The Soho Guggenheim looms into view
And it's more than worth six bucks to check my pack,
Spend the rest of this rainy afternoon
Absorbing deKooning's most famous works,
Impastoed and scribbled with black, carmine,
Streaked cobalt and deep murky ochres, mirrors—
Of what? Does that bent and fractured woman
Have a spine nibbled almost to lace by cancer?
Is that off-center, pear-shaped blot of red
The wound left by a suctioned embryo?
Can those eyes, bulging and hungrily feral,
See me, or beyond, to the smoked window?
"Art's no dictionary," a singer of this city—
Its happiest?—wrote. Nor well of sympathy.

7. Ann Arbor Variations

And yet O'Hara did collapse, and often,
My plane reading, a fat new bio, said,
Interviewing the hundred-plus best friends
He left behind. "We lose our health in love
Of color," he wrote when young and depressed
In Michigan, where K. feels down too:
Her spring break's to be spent nursing a cold
And divorcing, she sobbed on the phone,
Instead of meeting as we'd planned to do
For months. Huge bills come from their therapist,
Who twice had asked her husband "to the movies!"—
I'd meant to call K. weeks before, just check in . . .
Do we grieve most for those besides ourselves
When the heart warns we might be next in line?

8. Photography Wing

The teenage mother's face contorts with coke-lust
As she unzips the next john, reaching toward
His slumped back with her other hand; the infant
Grips both her leg and a ragged blanket,
The pacifier like a plastic kiss
That someone's stuck between his tiny lips.
"Don't go," I used to scream, "don't leave me here,"
When my parents drove off to dinners, furred
And tuxedoed; I tantrummed, held my breath
Until my blood-congested cheeks turned scarlet,
Almost as dark as the photographed child's.
Once I kicked through the glass front door, was held
For stitches in a sitter's plump black arms.
"Hush, mamma's coming soon." A false alarm.

9. Gramercy Park at Dusk

So much in New York is pure theatre:
That woman ahead, clad in lavish black
From heels to turban, walks twin terriers
Whose well-groomed fur sheens blue; the leash goes slack
Then taut as their legs lift to spray jonquils
That someone's planted by the curb. Her mink
And sunglasses, unnecessary props
At this time of day, in the heart of spring,
Disappear beneath a just-lit marquee
That's replaced my favorite hotel's awning
Since last year's stay. I saw it on TV:
The fabric cruelly rent, a doorman hosing
Pooled blood, the crowd drawn by her balancing act.
"I'll jump!" she'd screamed from the sill. Two guys clapped.

10. Another Saturday Night

The rooftop party's going strong at three
With "Layla" and "Suite: Judy Blue Eyes,"
Songs flashbacking those years of junior high,
The cool stoned boys, their girlfriends silent queens—
Parental battles, or was it just shyness,
Locked me in my room most nights with books,
Wanting Anne Frank's attic life, without the knock,
Of course, that made her drop her diary
To take any loved one's hand. . . . Laughable
At best, my small suburban fears and shames;
But what terror freights our early steps from home,
From families we're born to, none untroubled,
And toward these larger ones we make, messy
As the first with love and loss, our fumbled histories.

in memoriam Lynda Hull

OBJECTS OF DESIRE

The fish-eye lens warps Halliwell's face, pale as milky pudding
       Above pajamas
Sticking to his chest in a collage of blood and torn cotton,
       A surface fractured
Like the walls of their Islington flat, its bright kaleidoscope
       Of movie idols,
Tinfoil stars, postcards and dress patterns. Fractured like Joe Orton,
       Whose body lies smashed—
Lover Kills Playwright—by a hammer, swung to avenge failed art,

Failed love. So many betrayals. Past his stained hands, Halliwell stares
       To see Orton's face
Half-shadowed in public lavs; who hasn't craved a stranger's mouth
       Whispering come-ons?—
You're gorgeous, I'll love you always, you're still young. How do I look?
       Asks Vivien Leigh
In *Streetcar*, her wig the same ashen shade as Stanley's t-shirt,
       Sweaty and stuck to
His chest's muscled splendor. *How do I look?* asks Vivien/Blanche,

The fading belle who won't venture out till dark, who hangs lanterns
       Made from rice paper
Through Stanley and Stella's rooms; *how do I look?* till he rapes her
       And she goes insane.
Islington's now chic, Desire's now a project so dangerous
       Not even cabbies
Will go there. *Goddamn niggers'll kill you soon as look at you*—
       The fat driver snarled,
And I recoiled, though not like that British pair when they'd be called

Nancy boys, flounces, pud-lickers. A princess, my mother says,
       You'll look as pretty
As a princess; her curling iron scalds my ear, and I'm all shrieks,
       Wriggling to escape
Her hands and that frown, mirrored for whole days while my father's gone,
       Whole dusks of vodka

And ivory face powder thickening their silks. From the spare bathroom,
      Loretta calls, done
With the laundry and ironing; and how I love to help her dress

For these weekend evening dates: wide lips reddened between two curls
      Spit-wet and sticking
To her cheeks, she swirls conked hair into a lavish pompadour,
      Sucks her breath in hard—
Zip me, sugar-face?—as I tug and breathe the scent of lilies,
      A perfume that fades
When she leaves me to fishsticks and milk. And old TV movies,
      Or tearing through *Vogues*
To save pages for that year's best friend, whom I sneak out to meet

At his playhouse, darkly-shadowed till he rigs paper lanterns
      With flashlights. One shines
On his ash-blonde wig when he drops his coat, displays a costume
      Stitched from patterned scarves
Found in his sister's room, his mother's silk pajamas glistening
      Like both sweaty cheeks,
Glued with stars. Between *Reflections* and *Stop! in the Name of Love*,
      He swings the foil mike,
Smashing the air; he calls me *sweetheart*, he asks *How do I look?*

BLOOD ORANGES

1.

The inn's shuttered against Ávilan noon,
Against a pale, inquisitorial light
That nothing escapes on this windy plain
Where angels swirled into Teresa's dreams,
Such holy dreams her raptured limbs convulsed.
Pain's arrows broke through my habit, and yet,
Receiving this sweetness, my blood sang prayers.
My dreams, less metaphysical, swirl fractured
With parrots clawing at a vendor's cage;
With black-chadored women, arms locked in pairs,
Who duck into boutiques while chauffeurs wait,
Their radios tuned to weirdly wailing pipes;
With Guardía patrols, holsters swung low
By machine pistols. Now the fan's blades waft
My dropped, still-blank postcards, and I want dreams
Of angels too, their wings hymning escape
From travel-smutted flesh, from legacies
Of shuttered rooms and Easter dresses stiff
With starch, the mingled smells of sour milk
And talc—*Those freckles, child!*—as Southern suns
Force dogwoods' buds to cruciforms. At dusk,
My mother and her widowed mother, aunts
Long-widowed too, bless rumors with veiled tones
While I spear carrots, hiding the orange cubes
Beneath my plate. Rumors of their small town's
Adulteries and wayward kids, friends clawed
By sickness—*eaten up, poor soul; they say*
Three months. Clocks chime and my legs twist, stretching
To reach the floor. *God is in the details,*
Teresa said, remembering the arrows,
Those small blood-leaking holes in both her palms.
Above us hang framed oils and photographs,
Their black-gowned women posed against live oaks
Still draped with Spanish moss and razoring
The darkened sky. *God is in the details,*

Said the saint whose corpse smelled of roses
After her death, whose severed hand was carried
Through the countryside *to touch the sick*
And make them whole. To raise the dead.
Though shy, invited to few birthday parties,
I've attended so many funerals,
Dressed in stiff-collared black, that I revise
My bedtime prayer, also terrified I'll die
Before I wake. Everything's inherited here.

2.

Take, for instance, those hummingbirds fluttering
Outside the Toledo farmhouse last week:
Wings zooming up and down, their thin beaks pierced
The cobbled path's geraniums, blooms red
As the birds' throats. Where that path lapsed to dust,
Wind hymned through olive limbs and the sky swirled
With silver-purple clouds, the oily hue
In El Greco's dreamed funeral, its count
And anorexic saints exposed below
Unseen, inhuman hands that leaked lightning.
Two wrong turns in the olive grove, draped with
Low fog that clung to grass and powdery soil,
Wet my legs to the knees; and I startled
A hare, frozen in the dawn chill as steam
Puffed from both our nostrils. *No blessings here,*
The wind translated, *except for those who watch*
The sun rise till the ground scorches and ask
For still more heat, for those who reach to stroke
That quivery fur, who seek delight in gorse
And trampled poppies, that tail's uplifted flash.
Jet-lagged and lost in the dense-misted grove,
A near-hallucination of scrawny trunks
With dusty, blade-shaped leaves, I stopped, wheezing,
To search for my inhaler, felt my heart claw
Its narrow cage of countably stark ribs
Till noises from the farmhouse—kettle-shrieks,
Pots banged against a sink—told me which way
Was home. For a day. I travel to make peace
With mine till I'm exhausted with strangeness,
With washing shirts in rust-streaked bathroom sinks
And the black aftertaste of bitter coffee,
With sneezing fits mimed nightly for housemaids—
Habla inglés?—who bring more feather pillows
And stare like stones. The cobbled path grown hot
Beneath their crimson throats, the blurry wings
As darkly translucent as mourning veils,
The hummingbirds hurt each other away
From those blossoms with rapier beaks, also

Their tiny claws. But sharing doles of grace,
Small bits of heaven's dust drifted to earth,
Is unknown in the animal kingdom
As in childhood's domain: *you touch my blocks,*
My dolls, my collection of butterflies,
And I'll tell, I'll smash what you love, I'll kill you.

3.

For Lorca, flight to Andalusía
Brought neither lost youth back nor shelter from
The war, but only bullets splintering
The dust-veiled olive trees—whose childhood blessings
Were more bloodily mixed? On the dawn train,
I lapsed from views of his sun-fractured landscape
To a nap's dreams swirled by his aunt, reborn
As the black-habited Bernarda Alba,
Who shuttered her windows against the sun
And stars, who insisted her girls die virgins.
Her homely scepter's law knocks even here:
Streets jammed with late diners, with kids who spill
From Madrid's pulsing clubs to jostle those
Still hawking Marvel comics or mantillas.
Or toy machine pistols. Or rabbits' feet.
Or the next booth's drag-sized black lingerie,
Which two skateboarder boys poke sneeringly.
Their words aren't in my phrasebook, but recalled
From Lorca's gorgeous, self-hating tirade
Against Manhattan's sidewalk queens: *cancos,*
Maricas. Back at home, we drawl the name
Of our own *Andalooo-shha,* a town near where
En Sangre Fría's author, his cherub's face
Still pretty on the next booth's paperbacks,
Was raised by aunts who called him *sissy-britches.*
Later, he felt more at home with murder
Than small-town Southern life, despite a love
For its landscape, the oaks silvered with heat
And hanging moss that draped my early dreams
Of heaven. Some find it on earth, he wrote,
In windows filled by jewel-stained light, a light
Suffusing grace through cities yet unknown.
Miss Holiday Golightly. Dead Lorca fell
Beneath smoke-pluming guns; Tru's last book bore
Teresa's words about unanswered prayers.
What do they share, and I with them, beyond
A language of desire and shame, of homes
Escaped then mourned? Andalusían oranges—

I buy a bag, their scent acidly sweet
Through waxed paper, sweet as envisioned love
Made real. Why travel except this desire
For linkage, even skewed; its fruits blessings
We've dreamed foreign, their varied tastes received
And welcome as this blood orange leaking its sting
Down my square, freckled, inherited chin?

III

Following Signs

Only others save us, even though solitude tastes like opium.
Adam Zagajewski

HOME THOUGHTS FROM ABROAD

1. Reunions: Kensington 2004

Jet-lagged, yanking my mother's huge suitcase
Like a leashed and mutant dog, I stumble
Through the jammed lobby, a chill morning haze
Sooting the V & A's imperious walls
Beyond a bank of windows. "We're headquarters,"
The clerk explains politely when I ask
Who all those loud gray-haired Americans are,
"For the 82nd Airborne." First I'm blank,
Then alarmed—war again, and this one fought
By those nearing death, as Rousseau suggested,
Our hotel commandeered for drills and cots?
"Their reunion," the clerk adds, and how stupid
To forget D-Day's 60th, how vets
Would come in swarms. No rooms are ready yet.

2. Announcements: Jackson Boulevard 1967 and 1980

"I hate babies—they mess up your nice things,"
My mother shrieks, my brother spitting up
On her bed's counterpane, hand-tatted lace.
And like her china, even her wedding ring,
Among the last heirlooms long ago shipped
From a parent country that preferred nannies
And marriage for bloodlines, not happiness.
My mother's was "beneath her, a disgrace,"
Said a great-aunt once, half-drunk on sherry.
How long before their unblessed love turned bitter?
Rigid beneath blankets, I pray that they'll divorce
Through years of long wall-trembling arguments.
The night I tell my mother I'm engaged,
She cries, of course, and offers me her ring.

3. Half-Day Bus Tour: London, 2004

Our guide has told the joke a thousand times,
Sir Winston's drunk retort to Lady Astor,
Her ugly forwardness a female crime
In any century. "Victoria,"
He points to a monument, "dressed in black
For forty years to mourn Prince Albert's death."
Next a story about Brits' love for pets,
But I'm tuned out, my attention distracted
By London's dusk-lit glow, till the punchline,
Something about wives and dogs, all bitches.
My husband's trampling down the Yorkshire dales;
What stories does he tell to gain strangers' smiles
There, opting for hikes, not museum riches?—
Here the loot of a hearthbound queen's empire.

4. Steward of the Signet Society: Boston 1985

"Larkin's dead!"—the escutcheoned door slams hard
Behind an undergrad who's six months late
With dues; his friends at the lunch table
Drop their silver forks, slosh tears and sherry
On the linen cloth I'll later have to wash
And iron. Fourteen grand a year, plus free rent
Right in Harvard Square—how could my husband,
A broke midlife 2L, and I refuse?
Modelled on Oxbridge literary clubs,
The Signet has a library, small bar,
Members who've perfected British phrasing—
"White coffee," "bonking her"—but that day flub
Quoting those poems that comprehend the heart,
How it craves love, also deprivation.

5. Portobello Road 2004

How I loathe shopping, especially in crowds,
My backpack so loaded with Mother's finds—
Tea caddies, butlers' trays—I nearly waddle
To the next stall; she fingers christening gowns,
Then, stricken by her childless daughter's wince,
Seizes on a gift of silver earrings.
"Victorian," the dealer swears, then bows,
And points to what he calls his china darlings,
A row of dolls so cloyingly sweet-faced
They're icons for this country's child-worship,
Still reeling from that gruesome railyard case:
Three boys, two murderous, their four hands gripped
On film. A quick parole, adoption offers.
Let them rot, I say. Weep for their mothers.

6. Jackson Boulevard 1972 and Fitzroy Road 1963

Both houses white, both haunted by Furies
Who took their revenge as good women do,
Not with guns or knives but black depressions,
One's hair falling lankly from an oven door
As hissing gas choked out her eulogy;
The other crying in bed through whole seasons,
Wearing the same nightgown as summer air
Sharpens into fall, as I learn Shakespeare
And history, also how to clean a house,
Make dinners for my brother and my father,
When he's not travelling; how to wash
And iron between problems for geometry.
My favorite book in high school? *The Bell Jar.*
Recurring nightmare? Sheets stained, her wrists slashed.

7. Tom and Viv: Jackson Boulevard 1973 and Piccadilly Cinema 2004

"To be moral, I suppose,"—here Dafoe,
Who plays Eliot, looks upward from the rug
As though God dwelt within the chandelier—
"One must first be damned." The film gets better,
But the marriage can't survive Viv's bloody rags,
Head-blurring pills quacks said would stanch the flow
That continued red for weeks. She sniffed ether
And gave her husband his best Cockney lines:
What you get married for if you don't want
Children? At sixteen I knew what I wanted:
To be Prufrock, remote from those women,
Pliant and perfumed, whose arms were downed with hair;
To write poems singing as Eliot's dry bones—
Viv, a faithful wife, died in an asylum.

8. Westminster Abbey 2004

Just a few minutes until evensong:
Poets' Corner closed, I buy a brass rubbing
Of Shakespeare, whose remains lie undisturbed
Elsewhere, if grave robbers still fear curses,
The anger of the dead come home to roost.
Head bowed over packages, the hard pew
Surely spasming her back, my mother
Doesn't move as the black-robed junior choir
Processes. How tired she looks, and worn,
As I slip in beside her; the loft's organ
Sounds "Love Divine, All Loves Excelling," which soars
Above the cracking voice of one young tenor.
She pats my hand, smiling; God, what forms can
Love take except the smudged, the failed, the human?

9. The Tower 1986 and 2004

The Thames whitecapped: wind stands our hair on end,
Drowns out the Yeoman's spiel and the clamor
Of ravens we're warned not to touch: they bite,
Perhaps exacting payment for those clipped wings,
Which ensure they'll stay put and the Tower
Never fall, still faithful to the legend.
My husband, who brought me here on a past visit,
This year wanted our vacations kept separate,
His treks remote. The Yeoman defends Richard,
A hunchback but no killer: "cripples were feared"—
Mother and I bend under low ceilings—
"Being thought to bear the mark of Satan."
Some marks don't show. The crippled heart resists
The world—but how sick I am of prisons.

10. St. Paul's 2004

Public and various as a shopping mall
At home, with as many knick-knacks for sale—
Probably Churchill's turning in his grave,
Which isn't here, just a slab of marble
Marking where his coffin stood. Mother soaks
Her aching spine at the hotel, too tired
For any more cathedrals, wanting to pack.
An ill-scheduled group of Germans, guided
To the American chapel—Churchill,
Half-Yank himself, turns again—hears its words
Of thanks translated, and I want to kneel:
How is a free life born? *Praise Him, All Ye Works
Of the Lord* arches overhead in Latin.
I ask for blessing in my mother tongue.

AFTERWORDS

Your latest postcard's glossy lupines spike
In high-pitched hues: "powder puffs," you'd describe them
If, between acts, we sipped red house wine
By a glass wall, smoke blurring in stained plumes,
"For dens of vain wildlife." I'd grin, surprised,
As always, to recall your size-12 tracks
First loped Ohio fields. Sly, you'd revise:
"For female masochists, or do you think
That's a tautology?" O arias
Of laughter. O arias and arteries
And let's howl at the present tense. At this
Last card, a bad joke best cracked *sotto voce*
By some gout-ridden, nameless demotee
Whose age-diminuendoed range has chewed
At his career. Are *career* and *caries*
Unfriendly cousins to "decay," black snood
Of the same hue as Death's stained robe? And *care*?
And what of *carnivore*, that scene-chewer
Who prowls through flora glossy as this card's,
Mailed the day you died? Both of us were suckers
For etymology, still-hungry orphans
Like those two straining for the wolf's stone tits,
Mouths open and now art. O origins
And terminals, after *Terminus*,
The god of borders: those between close friends
Who mute a howling loneliness with cards;
Those, too, between the tame and wild. Dusk-stained,
My kitchen's perfumed with small reddish shards
Of Puppy Chow, and now the gluey smell
Of tear-blurred mail. "The hour of the wolf,"
Said forebears after learning to encircle
Their villages with walls: the dusk-lit gulf
Where housepet and killer become the same—
O arteries o howl o terminus—
As flowers and teeth, or flesh and its shade.

in memoriam William Matthews

CHURCH OF JESUS WITH SIGNS FOLLOWING
—Glen Summerford, Pastor

"They shall take up serpents; and if they drink any deadly thing, it shall
not hurt them; they shall lay hands upon the sick, and they shall recover."
Mark 16:18

1. His Wife, Darlene

"*A tongue like a black adder's*, he'd tease me
That first summer we courted. Smart-mouthed but shy,
I was the baby, raised with five brothers
Who pinched me during grace, knowing the yowls
Would get me whipped; stole my underpants
To trade for baseball cards with the McBees
Across the road; broke dolls' arms and my tea set;
Made a game of rolling me beneath the porch
And locking the latticed gate. *Ssss—gotcha—*
When their long arms poked, I'd get so wild with fright
That the crawl space's scattered kindling looked
About to coil and strike. That July noon
An arm wavered, heat-lazy, I sank my teeth
Into its flesh until I tasted blood,
Till Walter Joe punched out the wooden gate
With his other fist, the rest skittering like hens
As he screamed words that Mamma wept to hear.
Twelve stitches at the hospital; later,
Through a cracked door, I saw my daddy's belt
Cut his pale rear. Glen's hands were soft, their nails
White-mooned and clean; ten years older, he prayed
Farmwork wasn't his call. We drifted back
And forth in the glider all summer long,
And the night I shed my sass like outgrown skin,
He stroked my cheek and gave me my first kiss.
Pulled down onto his chest, I let my eyes
Take a slow wander past that thin shoulder
To our porch's warped boards, and, I'd swear
On stacked Bibles, their black gaps hissed a warning."

2. Back for the Wedding

Tense pilgrim speeding toward the rural turf
Of a future sister-in-law, I smirk
At my home state, abuzz with this trial:
The radio offers on-the-spot coverage
And expert panels, DJ's cracking jokes.
When the dozen grimy skyscrapers and steeples
Of Birmingham, my customary stop
For family dos, poke beyond the hills,
A nasal bass twangs a just-cut ballad
That cashes in on this snakehandling preacher
Who keeps his trade's sibilant tools at home.
What more perfect murder plan?—a wife
Held at gunpoint and forced to stick her hand
Into that basement cage; the lethal bites,
Glen planned, would be blamed on her lapse from grace.
Before his arrest, the faithful gathered
To hear about backsliding and backtalk,
Those idle mornings at the beauty parlor,
A jaunt to Atlanta. *Cherchez la femme*:
Two days before, the defense's star
Reported loud delirious prayers she'd heard
Outside the bitten wife's hospital room:
Darlene herself had opened their front door
To Satan, felt rattlers' fangs sink righteously
Into her arm while messing with the cage,
Wanting to give Glen a new plaything for bed.
Darlene rarely slept there, gossips said:
Only one child, and him now turned sixteen.

3. Suffer the Children

"*The Devil's Music*, Daddy called it, knocked
The radio to the ground and called me worse
Before loosening his belt. But he loves me:
A man and woman granted sons are blessed,
The Bible says, although made ripe for grief.
Once when I sassed him, bragging of a future
With my guitar, girls throwing underpants
And keys onstage, Jack Daniel's by the case,
He raised welts on my naked ass, then fell
Onto his knees and cried, confessed to whores
And puking beer; the young wife he'd beat up;
His time in jail for stealing rich folks' silver.
Poor Mamma looked sixty when barely half that:
Six bloody miscarriages; no money
For lunches at Woolworth's with the few friends
She had. Where did she get those odd dollars
To pay for my secret guitar lessons,
My secret dates? Daddy ripped the phone out
Last spring, ranting about women's tongues
And wickedness, but I'd seen the warning
From Southern Bell and knew his big-shot bluster
Had another cause. It's hard to be thankful
For greasy beans, harder to be a shepherd
When all you've got is goats on piss-poor land
Growing more rocks than wheat, those winter bucks
From ringing sales at Mr. Burns's store.
I called home when that social worker asked
How long they'd been married. *Near twenty years,*
My mamma sobbed into the phone before
The line clicked. Two lifetimes spent in prison."

4. The Reverend

"Look at these teeth, rotted by words that dripped
With honey, words the devil spoke in dreams,
Behind my mirrored face to teach me all
His names: six-packs of beer and trashy women;
Small change from burglaries; a father's pride
Lapsed to too much rod; that teenaged wife
Who sat alone in the front pew last summer
With a lace handkerchief for blotting sweat
Between her breasts. *Better marry than burn,*
Paul's letter warns, though weren't those martyrs made
Ready for God by brands and stifling cells?
My own, seven by ten, should give some refuge
From the world's vain array, its dull lawyers
And gossips, but even the prison dentist
Pokes into more than just my mouth—I swore
In court to tell the truth, and before then
To my jam-packed parishioners, preaching
From the wooden pulpit that Walter Joe, my son,
Helped me to build; they prayed loud for the call
To stroke my cage's hot-fanged offerings,
To conquer their unwilling flesh. I'll kneel
When I'm set free, to ask God not for vengeance
But for grace, to heal my wife's long-festered soul.
Turn the other cheek, says Jesus in red print
That blurs when my eyes wander to those pictures
I've thumbtacked on the wall: Darlene in white
Just after we'd vowed love till death; the other
An AP photo. Smiling sweet in court,
She climbed up to the witness stand in pearls
And a pink dress, then lied through her teeth."

5. Back

The jury's out, yet even after hours
Of switching between updates and talk shows,
A courthouse interview, I'm still unclear ·
Who tried to kill whom. One thing for sure—
Backsliding's serious stuff in Alabama,
But isn't that why I return? Too little,
Say Mother's phone calls and the creeping guilt
My entrance at this wedding, air-kissing aunts
And Junior Leaguer cousins, should absolve.
Southeast of Montgomery, through the bite
Our state takes into Georgia, a cross towers
Almost twelve feet high, its words demanding:
"Where will you spend eternity?" But hell—
I chafe at yearly leases, move so often
My china set consists of three's remnants;
The heirloom tea pot probably lies shattered
In a still-unpacked crate. The nuptial luncheon—
Did I RSVP?—already missed,
I floor the gas to keep my promises
To arrive before the preacher, to be nice
Around my blustering, off-the-wagon father
And new in-laws, to wear a decent dress.
In our pew, I brush my mother's offered cheek
As she whispers a greeting then questions
The small town florist's taste: pink lilies tickle
A stained glass Jesus; twining through large sprays
Of drooped orange gladioli, white swathes of tulle
Repose as though flung by drunk ballerinas.
All's placed to prettify a tiny church
So grimly meant for business I expect
The minister to lapse into strange tongues
Or drape a cottonmouth on his shoulder,
But I'm shamed as he starts to speak, the fire
And kindly heart of Wesley proffering joy.
A union's made and blessed; tears on my cheeks
Astound me as much as my fantasies
Of staying in a Deep South pastel with spring.
I hug my brother and his bride, a home girl

Made good at college with the Chi Omegas
And a nice city boy, though moonlighting
To pay for gambles on the Crimson Tide,
He nearly flunked out twice. Ah, the family—
Mine's hardly a viper's nest. I've backslid
All the way through the state, wanting hands
To be laid on me, still following signs.

IV

Home Movies

HOME MOVIES

1. Christmas: Ext., Wide-Angle

A Dantescan pit, the city glitters into view
   As this climbing, unlit street levels off and curves,
Curves so sharply the odd gift, a book of photos—

Fin de siècle dead girls from police archives,
   Also silverprinted porn—thuds to the car's floor;
You're dizzy from brandied fruitcake and surviving

Another visit home and—stop. Aren't you bored
   With those family scenes, replayed so many times?
And "Dantescan" and "surviving"—can't you find words

Less grandiose? And yet who doesn't feel godlike
   Speeding on deserted streets, the gorgeous sprawl
Of city lights below, those skyscrapers spiking

At your feet? And how the sweeping eye's lust swells
   As your ears vibrate with the tape player's chords
Now thrumming, that post-punk diva and grunge pin-up girl

Who wails *yeah they really want you* in "Doll Parts."
   Not what you really wanted, the evening's first show:
Your parents' surprise gift of home movies, cartons

They'd saved for years and copied onto video;
   The cheerless opener showed a foundry burning down—
O dying town of Bethlehem Steel—and windows

Shattered, wooden rafters split and sparking flames,
   In one hour your grandfather's job gone
That Christmas Eve. And close-ups of his sister, the shame

Of her suicide just months away. *O dying town.*
   In which infernal circle did Farinata rear
His scorched and ash-smeared head to stare down at Dante

From the glowing tomb, ask *who were your ancestors?*
    Close-ups of a wedding cake. *Yeah they really want—*
You know about the singer's husband, dead now for years,

Another suicide, MTV still haunted
    By his ashen junkie's face, by barbed-wire guitar licks
And shots of his little girl, who dances frenzied

On legs as plump as yours were kicking in red socks:
    Santa brought one doll, but you'd asked for two,
And tantrummed—*I want to be the girl with the most cake,*

The tape goes—by the tree. *Yeah they really want you—*
    Who gets to wish-list anyone as parent or child?
An obvious afterthought, the book of ghastly photos

On the car's floor, late-arriving from hundreds of miles
    To this city's sunken glitter; yet you forgive
Distracted, distant friends more than your family. *Smile,*

They said: is that such a wrongheaded way to live?
    Dead girls and bad girls blur their singing answers
Like the city, like the last shot of clustered graves.

2. After Baudelaire

The beggar child mistook my bread for cake,
And I was glad to share my loaf with him,
Having travelled so far from native hates
And loves. My eyes grew vast as the sky's dome
In that picturesque land, its mountains where
Clouds floated at my feet, where the faint bells
Of invisible herds tinkled like prayers
And I watched a lake's deep black ebbs and swells—
"Cake," gasped the little urchin, as if hoarse,
And I offered him another slice, smiled
At his sweet greed till a shadow appeared,
As small, as filthy, his eyes and hair as wild,
To fight him till the prize was crumbs and dirt.
You! Hypocrite voyeur! Ma semblable! Ma soeur!

3. Antonioni's *Blow-Up*

Already dated when I'm in college,
David Hemming's bell-bottomed swagger
And talk of Nepal, the thick eyeliner
Raccooning his models: misogyny

Or a knight errant's heart makes him walk out
Of one shoot, leave the models standing there
With eyes shut, arms artfully akimbo, bare
Bony torsos thrust sideways as they wait;

Already dated, the Mary Quant bangs
And white lips of two Twiggy wannabes
Who haunt his trail. The three fuck like bunnies
In one scene. It's all in fun. He hangs,

In his swank Knightsbridge flat, not fashion spreads
Or even portraits of the most gorgeous—
What happened to . . . was her name Veruschka?—
But poster-sized shots of London's rag-clad

Scrounging for fish and chips in curbside bins,
Sleeping in tube stations, sleeping in parks.
(Film 301. Late '70s. No talk
Of homelessness except after hurricanes,

Those fires and earthquakes covered on TV.)
Sleeping in parks. In a green leafy copse—
Even then my brain translated *corpse*—
A body lies waiting to be found. What's real

But the shots developed in his darkroom,
Characters and props taking hazy shape
As fixative scents the air, as blow-ups
Reveal a splayed leg flattening grass, an arm

Holding a gun, a woman's frightened face—*there*—
Then dissolve to grains? Or is the body,
And the gun, a trick of light? I'm twenty,
Taking notes as if the world might disappear.

4. "Installation," Warhol Museum

Swelled to peaks, the hot tinted streaks of flame
On each black canvas—one hundred in all—
Cast their symmetric flares around this room,
Almost a textbook chart of the spectrum
Though in skull-rattling, postmodern hues:
Blues like cheap eyeshadows, or fake tattoos;
Reds metallic as Coke cans, vibrating greens
The color not of grass but of migraines;
Still the yellows, centered on one white wall,
Are three pulsing flickers like distant flame

From a plains campfire in the last century,
Its sparks glittering the hope-fevered ones
Who pick lice from blankets and pray, half-sleeping,
That tomahawks don't take their scalps; that spring's
Tornadoes don't burst down from clouds to rip
The handspun muslin off their wagon hoops;
Pray poisonweed won't kill their stark-ribbed horses;
Pray when they search for water at sunrise
That rattlesnakes don't coil their hollow bones
To strike. From later in the century,

Trapped in the palest set of flames, I see
An image reprised from that Christmas book,
Its silvery outlines blurred: the murdered girl
Who fled the prairies' brute smother to curl
Her hair and hang a mirror on each wall,
To raise her skirts for men who paid to call
Her sweetheart: she bought the fluttering curtains
And plush, now-bloodied chair with the reflection
Of naked backs. Sex, like pain, is work—
See how carefully her sleeves are rolled, see

Her bruise-splotched legs above the boots she saved
For months to buy. The photographer's hand
Casts shadows on his model, her name unknown;
Warhol's shadow casts its throbbing neon glow
On his silkscreened subjects, here still living:

Pink-suited Jackie, Truman and Marilyn,
Shorn Edie with her skeletal glamour.
More voices swell their purgatorial choir:
We prayed for sparks from fame's magic wand;
Poor faceless pilgrim, pray we shall be saved.

5. Against Aristotle

Margaret eats fried chicken with her fingers;
Mine pick at still-warm bread as a fresh round
Of drinks arrives at our plush booth. "The *ground?*"
She asks, half-giggling at my arguments
Against catharsis. She's a long-time believer,
Assuaged the loss of dolls or pets in childhood
With *Charlotte's Web*; on bad nights, she cried
At Wilbur's near-death, his eight-legged repriever,
And slept, soothed. "When my parents' fights got loud,"
I slur, "That pig made me sob worse: some days
I'd take my father's golf umbrella and crouch
Beneath the pine trees, pretending to be—
Not purged but transported!—a mutant snail
Or neon-capped mushroom. Some wine? On me?"

6. *Gone with the Wind*, Boston, 1967

The favorite book of Anne Sexton's daughter
Fills the screen decades after its première

And Linda's wide-eyed when Atlanta burns,
Those technicolor yellows, reds, and oranges

As brightly-hued as her mom's sleeping pills,
Gulped with vodka while Linda reads the novel

Aloud, ash falling from Anne's cigarette,
Ash falling on those war-smashed streets. Nervous,

So agoraphobic that she rarely leaves
The house when her husband travels—*flee, flee*

On your donkey—to sell his company's wool,
Anne's let her *Linda-Pie*, her first-born girl

Choose her own birthday gift, this movie outing.
What large children we are here. Now pouting,

Scarlett slaps Rhett in their grand living room.
Anne digs stained fingers into Linda's popcorn

And swills the orange soda she's spiked, sees light
Caress her daughter's flickered hair, sees Rhett

Carry Scarlett, who fumes and kicks, upstairs.
Life is a trick . . . Linda's half-transported,

Repeating lines with those figures onscreen
Till Anne's *shhh, shhh.* Her hand in Linda's popcorn.

Her hand between Linda's stiff legs at night.
Children forgive anything if hugged tight—

But like that? *Life is a kitten in a sack.*
Stubbing out a Salem, Anne draws her mink

Around them both and pulls at Linda's hand.
At home, champagne and cake wait, also candles.

7. The Pink Palace

Not quite heaven, Utopia Parkway,
Those rooms cluttered with movie reels, tin stars,
Antique maps hung above stacked dossiers,

And two bins labelled "Dolls." Against a door,
A battered TV tilts, the sound turned off
To remind Cornell—arthritic, snowy-haired—

Of silent films. Miles distant, at the Gulf,
I'm six years old, assembling paradise
From broken shells that washed ashore like gifts,

Although a sunburn glows its fevered outline
Beneath my gown. No one's wakened yet:
Beyond the rusted screens, the dawn's pink light

Tints the sand like frosting; the TV set—
Do they have cartoons here?—and its dials
Are low enough to reach. "B-movie actress

And buxom bombshell, Jayne Mansfield, has died"—
A crashed convertible on the highway
That leads south, her bleached and hair-pieced head

Torn from the rest of her. My small hands trace
Her smile in montaged clips onscreen as static,
Also white lines, erupt; outside, blue waves

Grow blurred with hungry gulls. Often awake
All night, and lonely, Cornell looks for stars
In pre-dawn movies, breakfasting on cake

And cherry soda, or skims his assortment
Of girlie mags, whose backlit, earthbound angels
Part their lips as if to sing. Their harmonies

Will link the constellations and seashells
His hands frame in fantasias, gifts often mailed
To actresses performing loftier roles

Than Jayne's best: *Love me. Make me seen and real.*
Near his TV hangs a box from years before,
"The Pink Palace"; and maybe Cornell sees

Another pink mansion, Jayne in her yard,
Bikini-clad, bestowing stills and kisses
On startled tourists. If I can see and touch her,

Can she really be dead, vanished to drift
Like Cornell's last angelic nudes, whose gowns
Float sheer and pinkly as dawn's cloudy wisps?

A good girl, I don't wake my sleeping parents
For an answer, or unlatch the screened door
And soothe my sunburn in that gull-scavenged ocean,

But play distractedly with souvenirs
While the sun rises higher, casts the outlines
Of those screens, rust-brocaded, on the floor,

Hot blurry boxes glowing like my skin.
A lone gull dives, his black eyes trained on fish;
I grasp a seashell, whorled and cleft and pink

As any human heart, and the roar slips
Those fragile borders when held to my ears,
Which pulse like the world, like its homemade gifts.

in memoriam Herbert Morris

V

Solos and Duets

Death—it is the opposite of desire.
Tennessee Williams

BEFORE THE FLOOD: A SOLO FROM NEW ORLEANS

Crossing Lake Ponchartrain, vertiginous, my hands gripped the wheel,
      And—I'd have sworn it—
The bridge beneath me swayed as a dented maroon Buick passed,
      Radio blaring,
Back seat crammed with children, the Madonna stuck on its dashboard
      Clutching a horseshoe
Of roses. Homelife closing in, I'd scrimped for this day away,
      Not expecting haze,
Heat already swathing the smelly narrow streets, their beer joints

And souvenir shops selling masks half-price after Mardi Gras.
      And not expecting
A clerk's "Don't go past Dauphin, don't go out alone at night" when
      I asked directions.
Wary at noon, I skittered down Bourbon, darting from strippers
      In round-the-clock bars,
Tassels swinging on their siliconed, sweat-beaded breasts, again
      When I saw a man
On his knees at the corner of St. Ann begging for mercy;

The same cry I heard at mass in St. Louis Cathedral, where
      A woman dusk-skinned
As Jeanne Duval sobbed the response, her accent thick as coffee,
      Which I sipped for lunch,
Skimming a secondhand Baudelaire. Such willing confusions
      Of love and disgust:
Ruby-like nipples, syphilis blooming inside her. Hooves clopped
      As a guide retold,
To couples lapsed in his buggy, the history of the convent

And its nuns behind stucco walls—but I'd prayed already, purged
      To bone in shelter
And safety, and now zydeco percussed, delta blues wafted
      Around the statue
In Jackson Square; a young mother balancing a cherub-cheeked,
      Drooling baby dealt
Tarot cards and told my life-story so truly I tipped her

Ten dollars with hands
That shook, then walked smack into two men swapping small envelopes,

Their knife-like stares no match for the Lady of Situations,
        Her stern-eyed blessing
From a card that explained a past, while confirming the future
        Was mine. "When I leave
This town. . . .," but not yet, though the cathedral bell struck its hour;
        I reversed my steps
To sprawl on grass, sniff azaleas, watch a film-shoot. Humid skies
        Haloed the city;
A man asked me directions as if I lived there. "When I leave,"

"Cocaine, lady?," "Want a good time, lil' sister?"—if I answered,
        Would I remember
These swells and surges back home, allow them to transform a life
        I can't bid farewell?
And how can we belong anywhere except by peeling shrimp
        And drinking cheap beer
Before divining the way back to our hotels, blurred copies
        Of Baudelaire's poems?
Pigeons' stupid cooing finally woke me; I rushed to make

The check-out time, filling two cracked glasses to rinse my parched mouth
        And throwing matches,
A sweaty nightgown in my duffle. Nearing the bridge, which looked
        More solid, somehow,
Than before, I pulled over, seeing a procession circle
        Raised white tombs then stop,
Jewelling one with flowers, and I joined a woman who opened
        Her throat to echo
And to celebrate loss in that city of flesh and the dead.

MATINÉES

1. PeeWee's Big Adventure, 1993

The theatre's dark. Onscreen, a couple sweats,
Limbs twined crazily atop a bed that looks
Loaned from the Playhouse: scattered bright pillows float
Like huge gumdrops above the sheets, unfocused
And milky. Paulie, as his mother calls him,
Curls in the row's last seat, his long hair wet
With Palm Beach rain, cheeks unpowdered, lips thin
And parting. Too original for raincoats,
He wears jeans and a Barney t-shirt washed
Soft as a child's pajamas. Which she's kept.
With baby teeth, report cards, and a stash
Of clippings to bring out for company:
Him. Twice yearly. Now a flashlight points down,
Cutting the aisle. The cop isn't clowning around.

2. Pretty Babies: Malle Festival, 2000

In her first film, Brooke Shields is barely twelve,
The same age as Violet, the Storyville whore
Whose cherry's sold to the highest bidder:
She lowers that swath of crimson velvet
To pose on a pedestal, waving sparklers.
Now Bellocq positions mother and daughter
On a loveseat's plush, tugs at one's camisole,
The other's pantalettes, wanting symmetry:
Black neck-ribbons, black hose rolled to the knee
Make the two look like sisters, one slightly older.
Brooke will grow rich modelling designer jeans,
Mrs. Shields permit other, longer nude scenes.
Bellocq adjusts the lens. Pretty Mamma glows.
Reader, hush your mouth. This is the world she knows.

to Jerry Wexler

THE TRIUMPH OF STYLE

A blond goddess at ninety, unrivalled now that Dietrich's dead,
      Her spotted hands clutch
A cane, though her legs—stockingless, blue-veined—look sturdy enough,
      Their hard roped muscles
Testifying to the German love for fresh air, pine forests
      With thick-needled floors
Right out of Hansel and Gretel, the world of *lederhosen,*

Lebensraum. She feels betrayed still, this glossy magazine says,
      By the investors
Who snapped their purses shut after a pistol kissed Hitler's throat,
      After Berlin fell
In a mangle of smoking concrete, after *Auschwitz, Belsen,*
      Dachau, that litany.
Now still-shoots are her forte: these Nuba tribesmen—some pluming spears,

Others dressing a lion's carcass—could be dark-skinned versions
      Of Aryan youth,
Muscular and schooled to conquer worlds, breed with lithe blond women,
      To ponder Wagner
While snow swirled outside, shattered from gables in red-tinted dawns.
      All's shattered tonight
In Miami, after a hurricane's spin through that city

Of slums and sugar-grained beaches, sky-high murder rates, Disney
      And the purest coke
North of Bogotà. Keening winds silenced murmurs from doorways
      Offering dreams that last
Through the next pipe, for the youthful gold chains and teeth, tennis shoes
      At two hundred bucks
A pop. Who blames their hoisting white flags on adolescence's

Battleground, their looks from mirrors to store displays, wanting to
      Be *wicked gorgeous,*
Wanting to lavish a project's tiny closet with leather
      And silk, to be famed
For having *style?* The *Times* photographer, his lenses trained on

Destruction's glamour,
Took the picture that caught my notice fastest: a mannequin,

Eyes thick-lashed, blown from a beachside Saks window, her wigless head
        Resting on pavement
While her pelvis held its thrust-out pose, arms still cocked and attached
        To bone-sharpened hips.
Leni's camera cocked upward, in its most notorious image,
        To heighten a man
Small above those Nuremberg crowds, stiff-armed and -legged with salute,

His platform's marble lions like Pergamon's. Thousands of mouths roared
        Fürher, swelling winds
That blew for six years. We mouth platitudes on nature and force,
        Turn up our noses
At Jeffers' adoring tales of vultures and murderous cliffs,
        But style's a force too,
As Riefenstahl herself would tell you, or the armed ten-year-old

Found looting a Gap store among hissing electrical wires
        And fallen palms, or
This mannequin, whose grainy portrait I've taped above my desk,
        Her vatic silence
Somehow louder than gales on TV, and full of the meaning
        Given ornament,
The cruel myth held inside those blind, mascaraed, staring eyes.

MUSIC CITY DUET

Frost threatens, and the windowboxes' begonias
Turn spindly; their red petals, seared with brown, spill to
This left-behind ladder and the porch below

While Kitty Wells sirens "Heartbreak USA"
From inside a passing, beat-up truck, which loudly backfires:
The driver's probably looking for the tourist route,

Its studio museums with Hank's rhinestoned guitar,
A piece of Patsy's plane. Another backfire, or—Christ!
Am I shot? Bullseyed in my still-mending heart?—

Twelve feet above the porch's petal-stained cement,
My hand grasps the suctioned hummingbird feeder
And I'm steadied enough to glance down at my breast,

Where your red shirt, also left behind, grows darker
With blood. The driver, circling, seems unarmed but confused
As the end of "Cold, Cold Heart" sounds: irony

And pain compete while I scan the backyard for clues.
A neighbor's kid at play with his dad's shotgun?
Gang snipers loosed from meaner blocks, as TV news

Warns us nightly, on the suburbs of a town
That's always shoved its need and rage behind cordons,
Or into songs first heard at cramped brown-bag clubs spawned

From laws against the flesh? Mine's more scratched than punctured,
But underneath red cloth and scars, the muscle pounds;
And the truck's in my driveway, "I've Got Your Picture"

Blaring. "Hate to bother you," the young driver shouts,
In ear studs and black jeans like most hopefuls who come here
These days, his wide grin shrinking as I wobble down

The rungs. "That shirt's a target for the little bastards"—

He points above a windowbox, and why didn't I
See the hummingbirds before? Their iridescent feathers

And crimson throats shine like the feeder's nectar, dyed
Bright red to lure them to my sill. One veers left
And beak-stabs a rival, who takes revenge then flies

Toward safety, like the many soon-rejected hundreds
Who scrounge for bus fare home from Music Row. The tapes
This kid's planning to pitch—"thanks, ma'am, for the directions"—

Include duets with his girlfriend; and as one plays
And he drives off, I'd kill to hear your voice, a year
Since I wept, curled on the floor, and drank to your betrayal,

Predicted by harsh lyrics that blossom with targets,
Lonesome Hank and Kitty reared in dirt-poor counties,
Patsy's God quicker with punishments than rewards

For folks who fly too high, wear their hearts on fringed sleeves
In smoky rooms of bourbon-nursing strangers who've frozen
The seasons' pangs, bled hungrily with natural grief.

ANTIDEPRESSIVE

In mid-February, who'd expect to find Chicago warm,
      Its sidewalks sun-lush
And swelled with noon crowds who've unbuttoned their coats, the breeze lifting
      The tails like dark flags,
Lifting two girls' hair, cut short and bleached *en vogue?* Voices lift too,
      Some choired in praise for
The gentling of winter's fist, this year brass-knuckled, your letter
      Grimly joked, its tone
Mostly flat as these natives' vowels, unlike mine in drawled requests

For directions. What will I say to you? Three more blocks to go,
      None with any sign
Of the ice storm that delayed my plane for hours, downed branches
      And snapped power lines
Throughout the South. Clutching your letter when we finally took off,
      I watched skyscrapers
Brighten then fade in frozen rain, in low smoky clouds drifting
      At one building's base,
Snagged at another's center. A slippage of squares and oblongs

In monochromed light: was this the vision that haunted Rothko?—
      The vast staircases
Of the Art Institute take me past a portrait of that storm,
      Those buildings sliding
Like dark doors which tempt everyone sometime: when songs beyond them
      Siren louder than
Kind voices, when the brain caresses thoughts of how many pills
      That bottle contains
Or how many shells gleam in the pistol's chambers. One more turn

And there you stand, slumped beneath *Resurrection*'s leering angel,
      The painting ascribed
By some to Caravaggio. *Art is long, but this botched life*
      Seems longer, you wrote;
My friend, how I want to give you a faith no one has these days,
      Usually not me,
Except when midwinter sun warms my palms, still stinging from ice,

A faith that could see
Neighbors and pals, kids spray-painting sidewalks, even what looked back

From mirrors, as worthy models of grace. *A life splits in half*
    When a marriage does—
Maybe it's stupid to think anyone leaves pills unswallowed
    Or triggers unpulled
Just because of pep talks beneath paintings, but I want to take
    Your hand and point it
To the disputed *Resurrection*, those background crosses dark
    While that angel leers,
Suggesting fruit, lots of wine, and as for later, his brother. . . .

Sure, it's just art, but he stands posed in air warm enough to go
    Without coat or shirt,
And who really cares if the story's not true and the piece forged
    By a wannabe
Scavenging masters: the angel's mouth gleams above his grimed neck,
    Gleams in a blizzard
Of light, and urges large helpings, refilled glasses, making love
    With the windows raised
And voices too, in prayers for a lifetime of second chances.

SONNETS FOR TINA: A CALL AND RESPONSE

1. Tina in her Garden: Los Angeles

"Here love's got everything to do with it,
When sweat jewels between these crinkly eyes
And I'm wigless, singing beneath a sky lit
Bluer than blues, the clouds almost God-sized;
Beside palms, hibiscus, oleander,
All swaying neon-hued in weedless rows.
You'd think I'd hate dirt-work, after years
Of picking beans and cotton to buy shoes,
Cleaning up Ike's messes, but I'm queen
Of this ground, built this house, that closet
For silk and glitter, my own movie screen.
Mud streaking my knees or rehearsing new sets—
I'm both Tina, honey, and Anna Mae,
That nappy-haired child they all let slip away."

2. At the Tuckers: Ripley, Tennessee

My husband's birthplace ain't the bigtime, but
You called it heaven after sneaking out
Of your grandmother's shack that cold midnight,
Hoping the dog didn't loose a warning yowl,
The paper bag you'd packed a few clothes in
Didn't crackle and give you away. Give you away . . .
First Mamma, then Grandmamma, to her new "friend"
With sweaty, roaming hands that tickled like hay
Stuck to your dress. We walk next door and ring
Mrs. Tucker's bell, our usual Christmas call;
She's pale, half-deaf but cheery, reminiscing
About how she'd taken you in, lice and all,
As maid. "He don't beat you, that Mr. Tucker"—
Shyly, looking down—"Don't he love you no more?"

3. St. Louis, 1958

Bonnie Bramlett, later Delaney's other half,
Sings and dances, shimmies in a Dynel wig
And fishnet tights—the one Ikette not black.
Ike himself asked her mother's okay when that gig
Near the railroad tracks almost fell through,
Another defection. "I never wanted to be Tina"—
Then Little Ann—"In my wildest dreams, I knew
I could never be that good." But since her teens,
Sneaking across the river to the Harlem Club,
Bonnie Lynn had lapped Ike's sounds like honey
And tonight wears the eloper's dress, stuffed
With cotton wads for her flat chest and fanny,
Skin darkened with Man-Tan. "In the worst way,
I longed to be an Ikette." Even unpaid.

4. "A Fool in Love," 1960

Throaty contralto, your voice can peel wallpaper
And tells us you're nobody's fool, despite
The back-up girls' hammy doo-wop refrain.
Singing deep and rough, you're Ike's ticket out,
Out of East St. Louis joints, no locks
On doors, staying open all night, all day,
All year. At the bar, you sat with ankles crossed,
Prayed for your chance onstage, that ginger ale
Not what you'd come north to taste. How did things
Happen so fast? Soon you're curled in the same bed
Like sisters with Ike's wife, who couldn't sing.
Neither could Ike, recording moguls said.
"Just not his type of woman. I never was his type":
You never caught his eye, finally grabbed the mike.

5. On Tour with the Stones: England, 1969

"Mick never knocked, so I always stayed dressed,
But he's polite in other ways. I coached him
On high fives and hip swings, this funky dance
For white boys called the Pony. *That's rhythm?*
I teased, his skinny body strutting stuff
To mirrors, sweat shaking from his stringy hair,
Splotching crushed velvet britches that thrust
This way, then that." For once Ike didn't care.
For once my teen god wanted more than quickies.
"He wanted to *be* Tina Turner," Keith said.
"Still does." Two years later, hot and raucous
In Oakland, Tina brings to its knees a crowd
Mick called too stoned to move. For him, maybe.
Jumpin' Jack Flash couldn't top Proud Mary.

6. Nutbush, Tennessee

The sign's been stolen so many times no one
Bothers, or can afford, to replace it—
A place some Ripleyans call "Niggertown,"
Tarpaper shacks, mud yards, a lone juke joint.
Were you really foot-stomping for Jesus
At choir practice, just like in the movie
On everyone's lips this Christmas? My in-laws
Gather at the table, their Tina stories
Presented like the gifts we'll soon unwrap,
Most prefacing the "girl" you were back then
With "colored." On the drive here, we passed
The Turner Center for Domestic Violence,
Founded with your check. The Southern Family:
I keep my mouth shut, well-bred, cowardly.

7. *Gimme Shelter*, 1970

The band looks shell-shocked in this flick,
Scenes with lawyers and in the editing room
More plentiful than concert footage. Mick's
Shot backstage, checking out assembled groupies
While Tina does her set in lavender sequins:
Sock it to me, baby, she moans and gasps.
Cut back to Lucifer himself, explaining
"Something very funny always happens—
Please allow me—when we play that number."
Lank-haired, half-dazed with Percodans, my friend
And I lurch to the lobby to buy posters
Of Jagger's midnight strut. At Altamont,
Was he blind to bikers moving in to kill?
These days I sympathize less with the devil.

8. Re-Watching *Tommy*

Here's Ann-Margret, steel-coiffed and suburban,
Like my students' moms; though, for the wife
Of a British fighter jock, vapidly American.
Tina's needed to bring Tommy back to life.
She screeches: *this girl will put him right*
As her costume changes to spikes and steel bands—
This years before Madonna—just give her one night.
Deadheads grow fat with fuzzy good will,
Beatles' fans vegetarian, lovers of the Who
Now hope, before they die, they'll get old.
The Acid Queen swears *You won't be a boy*
No more to Tommy, drug-stupid, eyes wild.
What magic keeps you *young, but not a child?*

9. Duet at the Girls' School

Touring with a local gospel chorus,
The Salt and Pepper Singers, my friend
Belts out "Headin' for the Promised Land"
In her Christmas tape, and I'm so jealous
I could scream, heading nowhere in a life
And job gone winter-dreary while those voices,
Black and white, soar beyond gray skies.
"A Modern Cleopatra"—one prankster's choice
For the Shakespeare project I've assigned
Is this Tina poster unfurled for classmates
Who've written dutifully on lives and empires,
So young they think these both can be rebuilt.
But how can I fail her when that mouth almost sings?—
We build ourselves, and love ain't everything.

Diann Blakely's first collection, *Hurricane Walk,* was published in 1992 and cited as one of the year's ten best poetry books by the *St. Louis Post-Dispatch*; *Farewell, My Lovelies,* her second volume, appeared from Story Line Press in 2000. While still a work-in-progress, *Cities of Flesh and the Dead* won the Poetry Society of America's Alice Fay Di Castagnola Award. Blakely has also won two Pushcart Awards and appeared in *Best American Poetry 2003.* Having served as a poetry editor of *Antioch Review* for a dozen years, Blakely is the co-editor of *Each Fugitive Moment,* a collection of essays on the late Lynda Hull, and she continues to write for Village Voice Media and other publications. She lives south of Savannah with her husband, the author Stanley Booth.

Other Titles from Elixir Press

Poetry Titles from Elixir Press
Circassian Girl by Michelle Mitchell-Foust
Imago Mundi by Michelle Mitchell-Foust
Distance From Birth by Tracy Philpot
Original White Animals by Tracy Philpot
Flow Blue by Sarah Kennedy
A Witch's Dictionary by Sarah Kennedy
Monster Zero by Jay Snodgrass
Drag by Duriel E. Harris
Running the Voodoo Down by Jim McGarrah
Assignation at Vanishing Point by Jane Satterfield
The Jewish Fake Book by Sima Rabinowitz
Recital by Samn Stockwell
Murder Ballads by Jake Adam York
Floating Girl (Angel of War) by Robert Randolph
Puritan Spectacle by Robert Strong
Keeping the Tigers Behind Us by Glenn J. Freeman
Bonneville by Jenny Mueller
The Halo Rule by Teresa Leo
Perpetual Care by Katie Cappello

Fiction Titles
How Things Break by Kerala Goodkin

Limited Edition Chapbooks
Juju by Judy Moffat
Grass by Sean Aden Lovelace
X-testaments by Karen Zealand
Rapture by Sarah Kennedy
Green Ink Wings by Sherre Myers
Orange Reminds You Of Listening by Kristin Abraham
In What I Have Done & What I Have Failed To Do by Joseph P. Wood
Hymn of Ash by George Looney
Bray by Paul Gibbons